THE
WEIMARANER

by Charlotte Wilcox

Consultant:
Marge Davis
Secretary
Weimaraner Club of America

CAPSTONE
HIGH-INTEREST
BOOKS

an imprint of Capstone Press
Mankato, Minnesota

Capstone High-Interest Books are published by Capstone Press
151 Good Counsel Drive, P.O. Box 669, Mankato, Minnesota 56002
http://www.capstone-press.com

Library of Congress Cataloging-in-Publication Data
Wilcox, Charlotte.
   The weimaraner/by Charlotte Wilcox.
   p. cm.—(Learning about dogs)
   Includes bibliographical references (p. 44) and index.
   Summary: Introduces the history, development, uses, and care of this gray dog, formerly used as a hunting dog for the rich.
   ISBN 0-7368-0163-4
   1. Weimaraner (Dog breed)—Juvenile literature. [1. Weimaraner (Dog breed) 2. Dogs.] I. Title. II. Series: Wilcox, Charlotte. Learning about dogs.
SF429.W33W55 1999
636.752—dc21   98-37631
                                                                                          CIP
                                                                                          AC

Editorial Credits
Timothy Halldin, cover designer; Kimberly Danger and Sheri Gosewisch, photo researchers

Photo Credits
Cheryl A. Ertelt, 4, 6, 16, 24, 33, 34
Kent & Donna Dannen, 13, 14, 22
Mark Raycroft, cover, 9, 10, 18, 20, 27, 28, 30, 37, 38–39, 43, 46

2 3 4 5 6 05 04 03 02

Table of Contents

Quick Facts about the Weimaraner

Description

Height: Male Weimaraners stand 24 to 28 inches (61 to 71 centimeters) tall. Females stand 22 to 26 inches (56 to 66 centimeters) tall. Height is measured from the ground to the withers. The withers are the tops of the shoulders.

Weight: Males weigh from 65 to 85 pounds (29 to 39 kilograms). Females weigh from 55 to 70 pounds (25 to 32 kilograms).

Physical features: Weimaraners are lean, strong hunting dogs. Their hair usually is short and smooth. Some Weimaraners have long hair. Weimaraners have long ears that fold down. Their tails usually are cut off to about 6 inches (15 centimeters). Their eyes usually are yellow or gray. Their noses are gray.

Color: All Weimaraners are a shade of gray.

Development

Place of origin: Weimaraners came from Germany.

History of breed: Large, gray hunting dogs came to Europe from the Middle East. They were crossbred with bloodhounds and other European hunting dogs. The Weimaraner was the result of this crossbreeding.

Numbers: The American Kennel Club registers about 6,000 Weimaraners each year. Register means to record a dog's breeding record with an official club. The Canadian Kennel Club registers about 200 Weimaraners each year.

Uses

Weimaraners are sporting dogs. Some do police or search-and-rescue work. Weimaraners also are good watchdogs and pets.

Chapter 1
The Gray Ghost

Weimaraners (VYE-muh-rah-nurz) are known as good hunting dogs. They are alert, large, and strong. They have a great deal of energy. Weimaraners also have an excellent sense of smell. They can track animals or people by their smell. When trained, they also can search for illegal drugs or bombs by smell.

Hunting dogs sometimes do not make good pets. They are used to being with other dogs instead of people. But Weimeraners enjoy being around people. They make good pets and good hunters. When properly trained,

Weimaraners are alert, large, and strong.

Weimaraners are faithful dogs. They will protect their owners.

All Weimaraners are a shade of gray. They also have gray noses. Many Weimaraners have gray eyes. This has earned them the nickname "gray ghost."

The Forester's Dog

People in Germany sometimes call the Weimaraner "the forester's dog." A forester manages and protects the land and animals in a forest. Foresters sometimes search for lost people and animals. They might try to catch people who break hunting laws. Other times they must control wild animals. Many foresters in Germany use Weimaraners to help them with these tasks.

Weimaraners have the skills to assist foresters. Weimaraners are fast. They can catch poachers. These people hunt or fish illegally. Weimaraners are strong and fearless. They can protect people from wild animals. Weimaraners also are gentle. They can be friendly to the people who are using the park.

Weimaraners have earned the nickname "gray ghost."

8

Chapter 2

The Beginnings of the Breed

Large, gray hunting dogs first came to Europe around 1250. King Louis IX of France brought some of these dogs to Europe from the Middle East. The French king began to breed these gray dogs. He gave some of them to his family and friends.

Kings, princes, and wealthy people throughout Europe began to use these gray dogs for hunting. They also crossbred the gray dogs with other European breeds. For example, they bred some of the gray dogs

Weimaraners have long been used for hunting.

with bloodhounds. This crossbreeding produced excellent hunting dogs with a good sense of smell.

Prince Rupert von Pfalz of Germany received some of the gray dogs. In 1632, the prince had his picture painted with one of these dogs. The dog in the painting looked much like the modern Weimaraner.

Hunting Dogs

In the 1600s, only rich European landowners hunted with large dogs. They used these dogs to hunt large game such as deer, wild boars, bears, and wolves. They hunted these animals on lands they owned. Common people did not have this privilege to hunt big game.

In the late 1700s, hunting changed in Europe. Large animals such as bears and wolves became scarce. Rich people then hunted mostly birds and small animals. This was similar to how the common people hunted.

Most large dogs were not good at hunting birds and small game. Hunters started using

At one time, only rich European landowners used Weimaraners for hunting.

smaller dogs more often. But hunters occasionally still came across deer, bears, or wolves. Small dogs were not helpful for hunting these large animals.

The gray dogs that had been crossbred with bloodhounds were different. They were big enough to hunt large game. They also were good at hunting birds and small game. People could hunt game of all sizes with these dogs.

Weimaraners point their noses or bodies at game.

Breeding a Better Dog

Wealthy European hunters often kept many dogs. They hired people to take care of their dogs and hunting lands. They also hired dog masters who raised and trained the dogs in kennels. The hunters kept their dogs in these shelters.

Owners continued to look for better dogs for their kennels. They bred new dogs to improve the dogs' features and skills.

Some private kennels developed their own special breeds. Many of today's dog breeds began at those kennels. The Weimaraner is one of these special breeds.

Pointing and Retrieving

Some hunting breeds such as pointers and setters are good at finding game by smell. They point their noses or bodies toward the game. This helps hunters find game. But these dogs do not bring game back after hunters shoot it.

Retrievers are dogs that are good at bringing game back after hunters shoot it. But retrievers do not point at game.

Weimaraners are versatile hunting dogs. They point and retrieve well. They can hunt in woods, open fields, or wetlands. Their size helps them do many jobs.

Chapter 3

The Development of the Breed

In the 1800s, Germans began breeding Weimaraners. Most of this breeding took place near a German city called Weimar (VYE-mahr). At this time, Weimaraners were called Weimar Pointers. Only a few wealthy German families owned and bred Weimar Pointers. This group included Karl August, Grand Duke of Weimar and his friends.

The dogs of Weimar were among the best hunting dogs in Germany. The duke and his

In the 1800s, Germans began breeding Weimaraners.

In 1897, Weimaraner owners formed the Weimaraner Club of Germany.

friends did not share the Weimaraners with anyone else.

After the duke and his friends died, their families took over the kennels. These families continued to keep the Weimaraners for themselves. By the late 1800s, there were many Weimaraners in Germany. But they were still owned by only a few families.

The Weimaraner Club of Germany

In 1897, Weimaraner owners formed the Weimaraner Club of Germany. The club made a rule that only club members could own Weimaraners. People who wanted a Weimaraner dog had to join this club. But joining was difficult. The club chose its members carefully. They wanted to keep the club membership small and among friends.

Club members occasionally let people buy Weimaraners without joining. But club members always sold them neutered dogs. These dogs were given an operation that made them unable to breed. This meant that no one outside the club could breed Weimaraners of their own.

Club members enforced these strict rules. They wanted to maintain the quality of the breed. They did not want people breeding Weimaraners with other dogs.

A Search for Weimaraners

Until the late 1920s, only Germans owned Weimaraners. But a man from the United States also wanted to breed Weimaraners. His name was Howard Knight. In 1928, Knight asked to join the Weimaraner Club of Germany.

The German club members feared Knight would crossbreed Weimaraners with other dogs. They believed this would ruin the Weimaraner breed. Knight promised the club he would not crossbreed Weimaraners.

In 1929, the club allowed Knight to join. They sold Knight two Weimaraners. But Knight was disappointed. The German dog club sold Knight two neutered Weimaraners.

Preparing for War

Knight still wanted to breed Weimaraners. He wrote many letters to the German club during the 1930s. But the club still did not sell Knight Weimaraners to breed.

In the late 1930s, life in Germany began to change. The German government was

Until the late 1920s, only Germans owned Weimaraners.

Today, there are many Weimaraners in North America.

preparing for World War II (1939–1945).
German people worried about being bombed.
The Weimaraner Club of Germany worried
about their dogs. There were very few kennels
with Weimaraners in Germany. Club members
feared the Weimaraner breed might die out if
these kennels were bombed.

The Germans thought the Weimaraners might be safer in North America. In 1938, the club decided to send four Weimaraner puppies to Knight. These Weimaraners could breed.

Weimaraners in North America
Knight started breeding Weimaraners in the United States. He kept his promise to the German club. He did not crossbreed the Weimaraners with other breeds.

In 1939, World War II began in Europe. The German club then sent more Weimaraners to North America. Soon, many North Americans owned Weimaraners. The American Kennel Club began registering Weimaraners in 1943. The Canadian Kennel Club began registering Weimaraners in 1949. U.S. President Dwight Eisenhower (1953–1961) had a Weimaraner named Heidi.

Today, there are many Weimaraners in North America. The American Kennel Club registers about 6,000 Weimaraners each year. The Canadian Kennel Club registers about 200 Weimaraners each year.

Chapter 4
The Weimaraner Today

Today, people like Weimaraners for many reasons. Weimaraners are excellent hunting dogs. But they also make good pets.

Appearance

Weimaraners are known for their color. All Weimaraners are a shade of gray. This color can range from light silver gray to dark gray. Some Weimaraners have a small, white mark on their chests. A very small number of Weimaraners are a very dark shade of gray.

Weimaraners make excellent hunting dogs and good pets.

Dog clubs do not allow these darker
Weimaraners to be in dog shows.

Weimaraners have other interesting features.
Their noses are gray. Their long ears fold
down. Their eyes can be blue-gray or yellow.
People usually cut Weimaraners' tails to about
6 inches (15 centimeters).

Male Weimaraners stand 24 to 28 inches (61
to 71 centimeters) tall. Females stand 22 to 26
inches (56 to 66 centimeters) tall. Height is
measured from the ground to the withers. The
withers are the tops of the shoulders.

Male Weimaraners weigh from 65 to 85
pounds (29 to 39 kilograms). Females weigh
from 55 to 70 pounds (25 to 32 kilograms).

Short and Long Hair

Most Weimaraners have short, smooth coats.
But some Weimaraners have long hair. In the
1800s, breeders in Germany did not breed
long-haired Weimaraners. They did not want
them to pass on the long hair to their puppies.

But German breeders found that breeding
only short-haired Weimaraners caused

Most Weimaraners have short, smooth coats.

problems. Many short-haired Weimaraners were born with too little hair. They became cold easily. People in Germany used Weimaraners for hunting. They needed dogs with a warmer coat for hunting in the cold German climate. Breeders in Germany began to breed long-haired Weimaraners.

Today, only the United States and Canada do not allow long-haired Weimaraners in dog shows. But people also own long-haired Weimaraners in these two countries. Long-haired and short-haired Weimaraners both make good hunting dogs and pets.

Short-haired Weimaraners can get cold in the winter.

Chapter 5
Owning a Weimaraner

It is best to buy Weimaraners from breeders. There are Weimaraner clubs in almost every U.S. state and Canadian province. These clubs have names of breeders with Weimaraners for sale. People also can look for Weimaraner breeders at dog shows.

People who want to buy a puppy should first see both of the puppy's parents. This is not possible in a pet store. Most breeders let buyers see the puppy's parents. Breeders usually do not sell their dogs in pet stores.

It is best to buy Weimaraners from breeders.

Sometimes Weimaraners can be adopted. Breed clubs or rescue shelters may have information about adopting Weimaraners. Rescue shelters find homes for homeless dogs.

Adopted dogs usually cost less than dogs from breeders. Some adopted dogs are even free. Many already are trained.

Feeding a Weimaraner

The best diet for a Weimaraner is dog food. Pet stores sell several forms of dog food. The most common forms are dry, semimoist, and canned. Weimaraners can eat any of these forms.

Adult Weimaraners usually eat about 1 pound (.5 kilograms) of dry or semimoist food each day. Some Weimaraners eat four or more cans of canned dog food each day instead.

Weimaraners should not eat too quickly. This can cause a stomach problem called bloat. When this happens, the stomach fills with gas and becomes twisted. Dogs can die from bloat.

The best diet for a Weimaraner is dog food.

Weimaraners should have two or more small meals each day. This helps to keep them from becoming too hungry or eating too quickly.

Some foods are dangerous for dogs. Chocolate can be poisonous to some dogs. Dogs also can get sick from spicy or fatty foods. Small or sharp bones are not good for dogs. They can injure dogs' stomachs. Fish and chicken bones especially are unsafe for dogs.

All dogs need plenty of fresh water. They should be able to drink whenever they want. Weimaraners should drink at least three times a day.

Caring for a Weimaraner

Weimaraner owners must make sure their pets get plenty of exercise. Weimaraners have been bred to hunt. They can run through fields and woods all day long. Today, many Weimaraners live with families in cities or towns. Owners need to take them for walks each day and let them exercise in open spaces.

Weimaraners need regular exercise.

Weimaraners need a great deal of training. Untrained Weimaraners can cause trouble. Weimaraners need activities to keep them busy. Otherwise, they may become bored. Bored dogs may chew household objects. Some Weimaraners have even chewed their way through closed doors.

Weimaraners are happiest when they are part of their owners' lives. Weimaraners can make wonderful companions. Weimaraner owners believe their dogs are worth the time and effort spent to care for them.

Weimaraners can make wonderful companions.

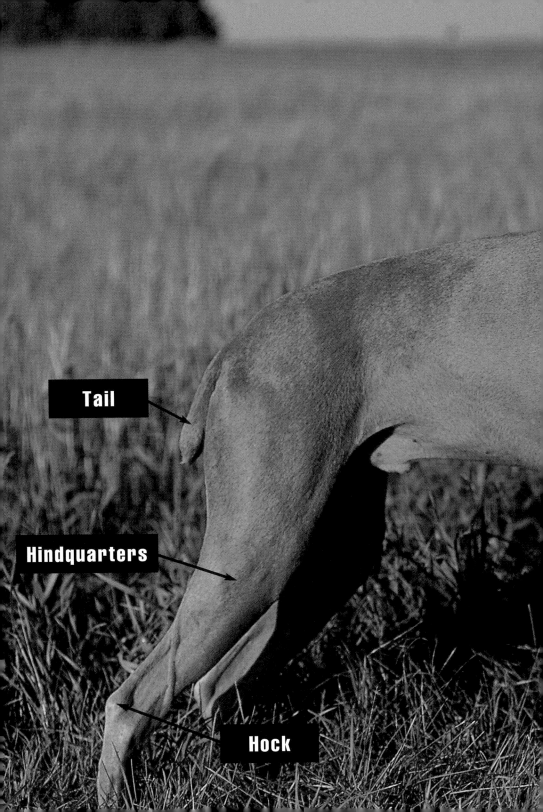

Tail

Hindquarters

Hock

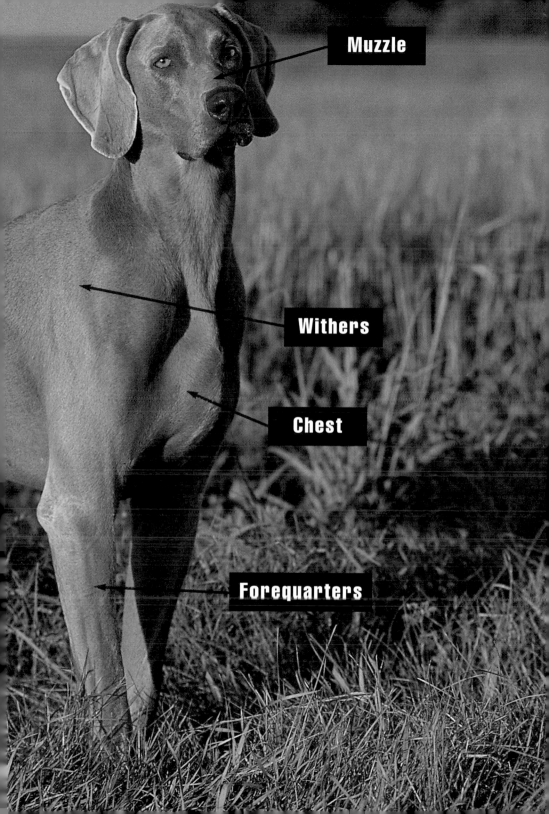

Muzzle

Withers

Chest

Forequarters

Quick Facts about Dogs

Dog Terms

A male dog is called a dog. A female dog is called a bitch. A young dog is called a puppy until it is 1 year old. A newborn puppy is called a whelp until it no longer needs its mother's milk. A family of puppies born at one time is called a litter.

Life History

Origin: All dogs, wolves, coyotes, and dingoes descended from a single, wolf-like species. Humans trained dogs throughout history.

Types: There are about 350 official dog breeds in the world. Dogs come in different sizes and colors. Adult dogs weigh from 2 pounds (1 kilogram) to more than 200 pounds (91 kilograms). They range from 6 inches (15 centimeters) to 36 inches (91 centimeters) tall.

Reproductive life: Dogs mature at 6 to 18 months. Puppies are born two months after breeding. A female can have two litters per year. An average litter has three to six puppies. Litters of 15 or more puppies are possible.

Development: Newborn puppies cannot see or hear. Their ears and eyes open one to two weeks after birth. Puppies try to walk when they are 2 weeks old. Their teeth begin to come in when they are about 3 weeks old.

Life span: Dogs are fully grown at 2 years. They can live 15 years or longer with good care.

The Dog's Super Senses

Smell: Dogs have a strong sense of smell. It is many times stronger than a human's. Dogs use their noses more than their eyes and ears. They recognize people, animals, and objects just by smelling them. They may recognize smells from long distances. They also may remember smells for long periods of time.

Hearing: Dogs hear better than people do. Dogs can hear noises from long distances. They also can hear high-pitched sounds that people cannot hear.

Sight: Dogs' eyes are farther to the sides of their heads than people's are. They can see twice as wide around their heads as people can.

Touch: Dogs enjoy being petted more than almost any other animal. They also can feel vibrations from approaching trains or the beginnings of earthquakes or storms.

Taste: Dogs do not have a strong sense of taste. This is partly because their sense of smell overpowers their sense of taste. It also is partly because they swallow food too quickly to taste it well.

Navigation: Dogs often can find their way home through crowded streets or across miles of wilderness without guidance. This is a special ability that scientists do not fully understand.

Words to Know

bloat (BLOHT)—a condition in which the stomach fills with gas and becomes twisted

bloodhound (BLUHD-hound)—a large dog with a wrinkled face, droopy ears, and a good sense of smell

kennel (KEN-uhl)—a place where dogs are raised and trained

neuter (NOO-tur)—to give a male animal an operation so it is unable to breed

poacher (POHCH-ur)—a person who hunts or fishes illegally

register (REJ-uh-stur)—to record a dog's breeding record with an official club

rescue shelter (RESS-kyoo SHEL-tur)—a place that finds homes for homeless dogs

versatile (VUR-suh-tuhl)—talented or useful in many ways; Weimaraners are versatile hunting dogs.

withers (WITH-urs)—the tops of an animal's shoulders

To Learn More

American Kennel Club. *The Complete Dog Book for Kids*. New York: Howell Book House, 1996.

Driscoll, Laura. *All About Dogs and Puppies*. All Aboard Books. New York: Grosset & Dunlap, 1998.

Hansen, Ann Larkin. *Dogs*. Popular Pet Care. Minneapolis: Abdo & Daughters, 1997.

Rosen, Michael J. *Kids' Best Dog Book*. New York: Workman, 1993.

You can read articles about Weimaraners in magazines such as *AKC Gazette*, *Bird Dog News*, *Dog Fancy*, *Dogs in Canada*, *Dog World*, and *Gun Dog*.

Useful Addresses

American Kennel Club
5580 Centerview Drive
Raleigh, NC 27606

Canadian Kennel Club
89 Skyway Avenue, Suite 100
Etobicoke, ON M9W 6R4
Canada

Weimaraner Association of Canada
4883 Torbolton Ridge Road
Woodlawn, ON K0A 3M0
Canada

Weimaraner Club of America
P.O. Box 2907
Muskogee, OK 74402-2907

Internet Sites

American Kennel Club
http://www.akc.org

Canadian Kennel Club
http://www.ckc.ca

Weimaraner Club of America
http://www.geocities.com/~weimclub

Weimaraner History
http://www.weim.net/hist.htm

Index